United States

Bright, Beautiful Map Poster With Learning-Rich,
Ready-to-Go Games and Activities That Build
Essential Map Skills

by Spencer Finch

NEW YORK · TORONTO · LONDON · AUCKLAND · SYDNEY
MEXICO CITY · NEW DELHI · HONG KONG · BUENOS AIRES

Teaching *Resources*

Cover design by Josué Castilleja
Interior design by Holly Grundon
Cover illustration by Bob Brugger
Maps by Jim McMahon

ISBN: 0-439-54047-X
Copyright © 2004 by Spencer Finch.
Maps © copyright 2004 by Scholastic Inc.
Published by Scholastic Inc.
All rights reserved.
Printed in the U.S.A.
4 5 6 7 8 9 10   40   10 09 08 07 06

CONTENTS

How to Use This Book

This book is intended to help students develop basic skills in map reading. By using the wall map and the reproducibles, you can introduce students to new map skills or reinforce skills that they have already learned. The wall map can be used to expand on what students learn in Social Studies class, or as an independent unit of map study. It is also an extremely useful classroom reference tool.

The teaching guide section is divided into three parts: Introduce, Teach, and Taking It Further.

◆ The Introduce section links the map skill with the real world and students' previous knowledge, and creates motivation for students to learn the skill.

◆ The Teach section provides strategies for using the wall map in front of the whole class. This section includes ideas for modeling the map skills as well as large-group instruction activities for helping students understand how to read different kinds of maps and use maps for different purposes.

◆ The Taking It Further section provides independent activities for students and often links to the student reproducibles at the back of the book.

The activities in this book can be used in any order. The selection of activities provides a range of content and skills that is central to the geography curriculum in the middle elementary grades. The wall map is a United States map, and the skills and activities revolve around this single map, although related maps appear in the reproducibles. Particular attention is paid to difficult map concepts, such as longitude and latitude. However, the goal throughout is to develop practical map skills for students that can link to their everyday lives as well as to show them that maps and geography can be FUN!

Getting Started

Here are a few quick ways to begin using your wall map.

Question of the Day

MATERIALS: copy of pages 15–16 ◆ a container

These questions are a great way to start a lesson or to quickly review some map concepts. You may want to read one aloud or copy one onto the chalkboard each day. You can also reproduce the pages, cut apart the questions, and place them in a container. You or a student can come up each day to take a question to ask the class. Answers are found on inside back cover.

It's Out of Here!

MATERIALS: copy of page 17

To get kids to really explore your map and to jump start thinking skills, try this easy activity. On page 17, each row lists four places, one of which doesn't belong. Read the four words to your students and have them use the map to figure out why one of the places you read doesn't fit. You can do one each day, or give a copy of the page to kids to have them complete on their own. Once kids get the hang of this, invite them to create their own "It's Out of Here!" groups to try out on classmates.

Five-Second Geo-Cube

MATERIALS: a copy of page 18, cut, folded, and taped to form a cube

This is a good activity to do when you have a few extra minutes before lunch or at the end of the day. Invite a student to come up to the map. Call out the name of a state. Then have him or her roll the cube. For example, if you say Texas, and the student rolls the cube so that the "capital" side faces up, he or she has five seconds to find the answer on the map.

Where Am I?

MATERIALS: copies of page 19

Provide students with a copy of page 19. Have them use the wall map to find the answers to the questions. Be sure to discuss their answers with them.

States and Capitals Bingo

MATERIALS

◆ copy of pages 20–24

◆ bingo chips (small squares of colored construction paper will work)

◆ envelopes

INTRODUCE

Discuss the symbol used on the wall map to indicate a state capital (*a star*). Ask students to name and locate the capital of your state. Then call out the names of other states for them to locate the capitals on the map.

TEACH

There are two ways to play "States and Capitals Bingo." In one version, students are given bingo boards with the states' names (pages 20–21). For this version, use the call list with the states' capitals. In the other version, students use the bingo boards with the capitals on them (pages 22–23) and the call list with the states' names. Make two copies of the call list. Keep one intact and cut apart the other one and place the slips in an envelope. Make copies of the bingo cards, cut them apart, and distribute so that each student or pair of students can have one. Distribute the chips.

Review the game with students. Tell them you'll be calling out a state (or capital), and if they have the capital (or state) on their card, they cover it with a chip. Explain that a winner has five covered blocks in a straight line (vertically, horizontally, or diagonally).When "Bingo" is declared, have the winner(s) come to the wall map and locate the states and capitals they covered on the bingo boards.

TAKING IT FURTHER

Have students use index cards to create flashcards to help them remember the capital of each state. On one side, they should put the name of the state and on the other, the capital. They might want to include an outline of the state on the side with the state's name. Encourage them to quiz one another.

Rivers of the U.S.A.

MATERIALS

◆ 4-by-6-inch sheets of paper
◆ colored pencils or markers

INTRODUCE

Remind students of some river-specific vocabulary (*source*: where a river begins; *mouth*: where a river empties into another body of water; *tributary*: a smaller river that flows into a larger one; *delta*: land made of silt left behind at the mouth of a river). Point out the Continental Divide on the wall map and explain that precipitation that falls on the east side of this line flows into the Atlantic Ocean, and that which falls on the west side flows to the Pacific Ocean.

TEACH

Have a volunteer find each of the rivers listed below on the map. Have students determine where the source of each river is; what tributaries flow into it; what states it passes through; where the mouth is; and what body of water it flows into. You may wish to have groups of students work together to create a chart listing all of the information they can determine for each river.

Rio Grande

Snake River

Arkansas River

Columbia River

Ohio River

Mississippi River

Hudson River

Red River

Tennessee River

Colorado River

Yukon River

Brazos River

Missouri River

PRACTICE

Have students create a postcard using 4-by-6-inch sheets of paper and crayons or markers. The postcard should show some aspect of the river of their choice on the front side, and include a descriptive note about the river to a friend or family member on the back. Encourage students to be creative with their postcard designs by making a decorative border or by dividing the picture into four frames, and by designing a special stamp for their postcard. Remind students to provide a brief written description of the picture on the back, too.

Lots of Landforms

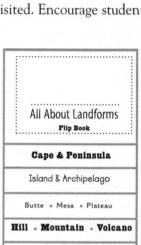

MATERIALS

◆ index cards

◆ double-sided copy of pages 25–26 for each student

◆ stapler

◆ physical map (optional)

INTRODUCE

Ask students to describe the landforms in the area where they live or in another place in the United States that they have visited. Encourage students to think about how different regions have different landforms that affect the way people live. Review with students vocabulary for landforms, such as *mountain*, *hill*, *plain*, *plateau*, *butte*, *valley*, *canyon*, and *mesa*.

TEACH

For this activity, you may wish to have a physical map of the United States available for students to consult. Tell students they will create a flashcard for each of the 50 states using index cards or similar-sized pieces of paper. Distribute several cards to each student in the class. Encourage students to look at the wall map (and the physical map) for clues about what kind of landforms exist in the states on their cards. On the back of the cards, have students write the type of landforms that exist in their states. They should write one or more of the following on the back: mountains, hills, plains, coast, desert, plateau, peninsula, or islands. You may wish to have them describe specific landforms, such as the Rocky Mountains or the Great Plains.

All About Landforms
Flip Book

Cape & Peninsula

Island & Archipelago

Butte ◆ Mesa ◆ Plateau

Hill ◆ Mountain ◆ Volcano

A Landform Puzzle

TAKING IT FURTHER

Provide each student with a double-sided copy of the "All About Landforms" stepbook (pages 25–26). Have students cut out the panels along the dotted line and fold along the solid lines. Have students slip the panels together so they can see the titles. Have them fasten the stepbook at the top with two staples. Students can complete the stepbook using information from the wall map, the physical map, and the flashcards.

The Most From Coast to Coast

MATERIALS

◆ small sticky notes or small pieces of paper
◆ poster tape
◆ copy of page 27 for each student

INTRODUCE

Take students on a coast-to-coast tour of superlatives—the highest, longest, oldest, tallest, hottest, etc., places in the United States. Remind students that the United States is geographically extremely diverse. You may wish to start by asking students if they know what the tallest mountain or longest river in the United States is. (*Mount McKinley is the tallest mountain and the Mississippi is the longest river.*)

TEACH

Write each of the superlatives below on a separate sticky note and ask volunteers to place the note on the proper place on the map. You may wish to add additional information to the note, with specifics about each fact.

Tallest Mountain: Mt. McKinley, Alaska (20,320 ft)

Longest River: Mississippi River (3,710 miles)

Largest State: Alaska (656,324 square miles)

Largest State (lower 48): Texas (266,807 square miles)

Smallest State: Rhode Island (1,545 square miles)

Lowest Point: Death Valley, California (-282 ft)

Deepest Lake: Crater Lake, Oregon (1,932 ft)

Largest Lake: Lake Superior (31,700 square miles)

Largest Population: New York City (8,006,278)

Rainiest Place: Mt. Waialeale, Hawaii (460 inches/year)

Highest Waterfall: Yosemite Falls, California (2,425 ft)

Longest Suspension Bridge: Verrazano Narrows, New York City (4,260 ft)

Oldest National Park: Yellowstone, Wyoming (1872)

Strongest Wind: Mt. Washington, New Hampshire (231 mph)

Most Tornadoes Per Year: Texas (average 139)

Longest Coastline: California (5,580 miles)

Northernmost City: Barrow, Alaska

Southernmost City: Hilo, Hawaii

Easternmost City: Eastport, Maine

Westernmost City: Atka, Alaska

Largest Gorge: Grand Canyon, Arizona (277 miles long)

First State: Delaware (1787)

Largest Desert: Sonoran (California, Arizona, Mexico) (70,000 sq miles)

TAKING IT FURTHER

To help students learn more about mountain peaks in the United States, have them complete page 27.

Creating a Climate Map

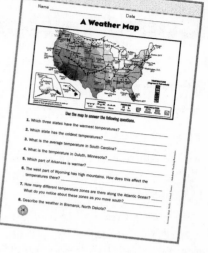

MATERIALS

◆ small sticky notes in seven different colors or small pieces of paper in seven different colors

◆ poster tape

◆ copy of page 28 for each student

INTRODUCE

Encourage students to describe the climate of the place where they live. Help them understand the difference between weather and climate, explaining that climate is the weather that a place has over a long period of time. Remind students that there are two main parts of climate: temperature and precipitation. Latitude, proximity to oceans, and elevation all influence climate.

TEACH

First, point out the key on the wall map. Discuss the symbols in the key. Then tell students you will create a climate map of the U.S. with a new map key that uses colors as symbols. On a large piece of white paper, place one sticky note of each color on the left side and write the following descriptions of the different climate zones next to each sticky note.

A) warm summer, cold winter, wet

B) hot summer, cool winter, wet

C) warm summer, cold winter, dry

D) hot summer, cool winter, dry

E) warm summer, mild winter, wet

F) warm and wet year-round

G) cool summer, very cold winter

Next, provide students with different-colored sticky notes and invite them to complete the map by placing the proper color sticky note on each state. (See chart on the left.) Remind students that some states, especially larger ones, fall in more than one climate region. You may wish to assign each student one or two states. Alternately, you may wish to assign a group of students to each climate region.

After the map is completed, discuss how the colors divide up the country into different regions. Point out how factors such as mountains and proximity to water can affect the climate of a place.

A) Maine, New Hampshire, Vermont, Massachusetts, Rhode Island, Connecticut, New York, New Jersey, Pennsylvania, Delaware, Maryland, West Virginia, Kentucky, Ohio, Indiana, Michigan, Illinois, Wisconsin, Missouri, Iowa, Minnesota

B) Virginia, North Carolina, South Carolina, Georgia, Florida, Alabama, Mississippi, Tennessee, Arkansas, Louisiana, Texas

C) North Dakota, South Dakota, Nebraska, Kansas, Colorado, Montana, Idaho, Wyoming, Utah

D) Texas, New Mexico, Arizona, Nevada, Utah, California

E) Washington, Oregon, California

F) Hawaii

G) Alaska

TAKING IT FURTHER

Have students complete page 28 to practice the skill of reading a weather map.

Latitude and Longitude Game

MATERIALS

◆ copy of page 29 for each student

INTRODUCE

Explain to students that every place on Earth has an "address." These addresses are formed by a grid of crossing lines called *latitude* and *longitude*. Point out to students that the lines that run horizontally from east to west are lines of *latitude* (also called "parallels") and lines that run vertically from north to south are lines of *longitude* (also called "meridians"). On the wall map, show them how the lines have numbers that get higher as they move north or west. This is because the United States is north of the *equator* (0° latitude) and west of the *prime meridian* (0° longitude). Explain that longitude and latitude are measured in degrees (symbol °), and that the latitude of a place is given before its longitude. To help students become familiar with these concepts, ask the following questions: Which line of latitude runs through the north part of Florida? (*30°N*) Which line of longitude runs through the center of Montana? (*110°W*) What is the latitude and longitude of New Orleans, Louisiana? (*30°N, 90°W*)

TEACH

Play a latitude and longitude game to help students deepen their understanding of the concept. Divide the class into three teams: Latitude, Longitude, and Location. Students from the Latitude team should write a degree of latitude on a piece of paper (making sure the location falls within the United States) and pass it to the Longitude team. Then a member of the longitude team should add a degree of longitude on the paper (again, making sure the location falls within the United States) and pass it to the location team. Then a member of the Location team should locate the latitude and longitude on the map and write the state where it is located on the paper. After they are complete, go through the papers as a class to check for correct locations. To create a competition, have teams switch roles so each team has a chance to determine location. Then time each team as it finds locations. The team that correctly locates all the points in the shortest time wins. You may wish to have students reverse the order of the game above by picking a state or city and then determining its location in latitude and longitude.

TAKING IT FURTHER

Have students complete the reproducible on page 29 to reinforce their understanding of latitude and longitude.

Regions of the United States

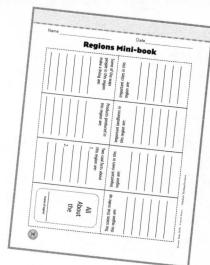

MATERIALS

◆ copy of page 30 for each student

INTRODUCE

Explain to students that a *region* is an area that shares common features, such as landforms, climate, or population. Geographers find it useful to divide the United States into different regions, and commonly use the following five regional names: Northeast, Southeast, Midwest, Southwest, and West.

TEACH

Write the list of regions given below on the board or on a handout to distribute to students. Then work together to complete a chart that describes some of the features that make each of the regions of the United States unique. Encourage students to look at the information on the map and to think about what they already know about the country's environment, culture, and economy as they complete the chart. You may wish to highlight the regions by color-coding states with sticky notes or creating regional borders on the wall map using poster tape and colored yarn.

TAKING IT FURTHER

Have students choose one of the five regions of the United States and create a mini-book about that region, using the reproducible found on page 30.

Region	States
Northeast	Maine, New Hampshire, Vermont, Massachusetts, New York, Rhode Island, Connecticut, Pennsylvania, New Jersey, Delaware, Maryland
Southeast	West Virginia, Virginia, Kentucky, Tennessee, North Carolina, South Carolina, Georgia, Florida, Alabama, Mississippi, Louisiana, Arkansas
Midwest	Ohio, Indiana, Michigan, Illinois, Wisconsin, Minnesota, Iowa, Missouri, North Dakota, South Dakota, Nebraska, Kansas
Southwest	Oklahoma, Texas, New Mexico, Arizona
West	Montana, Wyoming, Colorado, Idaho, Utah, Washington, Oregon, Nevada, California, Alaska, Hawaii

Using a Scale

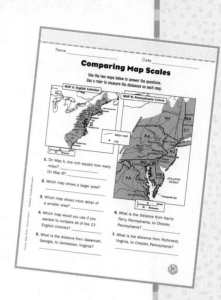

MATERIALS

◆ sticky notes

◆ copy of page 31 for each student

INTRODUCE

Explain to students that *scale* is the way to tell distances on a map. Scale is the relationship between the distance shown on a map and the real distance on Earth. Different-size maps have different scales. On the large wall map, for example, one inch equals 100 miles, but on a smaller atlas map one inch might equal 500 miles.

TEACH

Tell students that you are going to plan a trip across the country. The trip will take six days. Since the distance from coast to coast is about 3,000 miles, you plan to travel about 500 miles per day. Have a student choose a place on the East or West Coast to begin the trip. Another student can choose the destination on the opposite coast. Attach a sticky note and write "0 miles" and a description of the starting point. Invite volunteers to come to the map to use the scale to determine where the next stop on the trip might be. Add a sticky note to indicate each day's ending point. Students should continue to mark stops every 500 miles until they reach your destination on the other coast.

As an extension activity, have students write a one-page summary of each day's travel. Lead students in a discussion of the different routes across the country and what advantages and disadvantages the different routes hold as well as the sights and cities each route passed.

TAKING IT FURTHER

Have students complete the reproducible on page 31 to practice using a map scale.

13

A Population Map

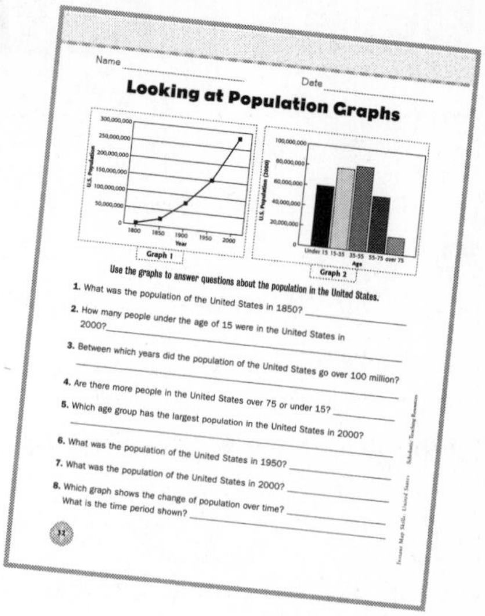

A partially visible reproducible worksheet titled "Looking at Population Graphs" appears at the top right of the page.

MATERIALS

- tracing paper
- crayons
- scissors
- poster tape
- copy of page 32 for each student

INTRODUCE

Ask students: "How can color on a map provide information?" Guide students to see that color can serve as a symbol on a map; for example, the color blue often stands for water. Explain that in this activity they will create a color code of the states to show the population of each state in the United States.

TEACH

Assign each student one or more states and provide each with a piece of tracing paper big enough to fit over their states on the wall map. (You may want to group some neighboring small states.) Have students trace their states on the paper and then cut them out. Using the key at left, have students color their cutouts with the correct color for their state's population. Have them write the state name (or abbreviation for small states) on the cutout in a contrasting color. Work together with students (or assign a group of students to this task) to create a key on a large piece of white paper, showing which colors stand for which population figures. On a large table, have students work together to tape the colored cutouts together along the borders in their correct position to form a patchwork population map of the United States. Carefully transfer the map to the wall or bulletin board and hang the key next to it. Use the map as a jumping-off point for a class discussion about population and geography in the United States. Ask students to describe where the most-populated and least-populated states are located. Ask them why they think some small states might have more people than some large states.

TAKING IT FURTHER

Have students complete the reproducible on page 32, which presents population information about the United States in charts and graphs. After completing the reproducible, ask students to describe how the graphs and maps present population data differently and how one might be more useful than the other.

KEY

More than 10 million: (red)
California, Texas, New York, Florida, Illinois, Pennsylvania, Ohio

5 million to 10 million: (blue)
Michigan, New Jersey, Georgia, North Carolina, Virginia, Massachusetts, Indiana

4 to 5 million: (yellow)
Washington, Tennessee, Missouri, Wisconsin, Maryland, Arizona, Minnesota, Louisiana, Alabama

2 to 4 million: (green)
Colorado, Kentucky, South Carolina, Oklahoma, Oregon, Connecticut, Iowa, Mississippi, Kansas, Arkansas,

1 to 2 million: (orange)
Utah, Nevada, New Mexico, West Virginia, Nebraska, Idaho, Maine, New Hampshire, Hawaii, Rhode Island

Less than 1 million: (gray)
Montana, Delaware, South Dakota, North Dakota, Alaska, Vermont, Wyoming

14

Question of the Day

1. What is the most eastern state of the United States?

2. What is the most western state of the United States?

3. What is the most northern state of the United States?

4. What is the most southern state of the United States?

5. On which continent is the United States located?

6. What ocean is to the west of the United States?

7. What ocean is to the east of the United States?

8. What body of water is to the south of the United States?

9. What country is north of the United States?

10. What country is south of the United States?

11. What are the names of the Great Lakes?

12. Which states border the Great Lakes?

13. Which Great Lake is completely within the United States?

14. Which mountain range runs from Maine to Georgia?

15. Which mountain range runs from Montana to New Mexico?

16. What is the highest mountain in the United States? In which state is it located?

17. What is the highest mountain in the "lower 48" states?

18. Which state is a peninsula?

19. Which state is an archipelago?

20. Which state in the "lower 48" borders only one other state?

21. How many states border an ocean?

22. How many states do not border any ocean?

23. Which states border the Atlantic Ocean?

24. Which states border the Pacific Ocean?

25. Which states border the Gulf of Mexico?

26. In which direction does the Mississippi River flow?

Question of the Day

27. Where does the Mississippi River begin?

28. Where does the Mississippi River end?

29. Which states border the Mississippi River?

30. Which national border is the longest?

31. Which states are located along this border?

32. The Rio Grande forms part of the border with what country?

33. Which states are located along this border?

34. Which city is located where 30°N and 90° W cross?

35. The 49th parallel (49°N) forms part of the border between which countries?

36. Most of the United States is located above which line of longitude? Which states dip below this line?

37. If you travel directly north from Louisiana, which state will you reach?

38. If you travel directly west from South Carolina, which state will you reach?

39. If you sail south from Miami, Florida, which country will you reach?

40. How many islands of Hawaii are shown on this map?

41. Which country is located to the east of Alaska?

42. In which part of the country is the nation's capital located?

43. Are the states generally bigger in the east or in the west?

44. Which river forms the southern border of Ohio and Indiana?

45. Which states border the state of Missouri?

46. In which state is the biggest lake west of the Mississippi River?

47. Which body of water borders Alaska to the south?

48. In which direction is North Dakota in relation to South Dakota?

49. Which two states are perfect rectangles?

50. Which four states meet at a point called "the four corners"?

Instant Map Skills: United States   Scholastic Teaching Resources

It's Out of Here!

One item in each row doesn't belong. Think about the choices and look at the wall map.
Circle the item that doesn't belong to show that "It's Out of Here!"

1.	North Carolina	South Carolina	New Jersey	Ohio
2.	Arizona	Kentucky	New Mexico	Utah
3.	Kansas	Washington	Florida	California
4.	Minnesota	Missouri	Colorado	Louisiana
5.	Wisconsin	Vermont	Maine	Texas
6.	California	Oregon	Idaho	Washington
7.	Ohio	Idaho	Colorado	Wyoming
8.	Oklahoma	Kansas	South Dakota	Rhode Island
9.	Arkansas	Connecticut	Illinois	Utah
10.	Tennessee	Michigan	Indiana	Illinois
11.	Texas	California	Arizona	Alabama
12.	Rhode Island	Hawaii	Delaware	Alaska
13.	Nevada	Idaho	Pennsylvania	Oregon
14.	Alabama	Florida	Georgia	Montana
15.	West Virginia	Iowa	Tennessee	Pennsylvania
16.	New York City	Salem	Lincoln	Sacramento
17.	Mississippi	Appalachians	Arkansas	Missouri
18.	Lake Huron	Great Salt Lake	Lake Michigan	Lake Superior

Geo-Cube

Cut out the cube along the dashed line and fold along the solid lines. Tuck the gray flaps inside.
Then tape the sides together to form a cube.

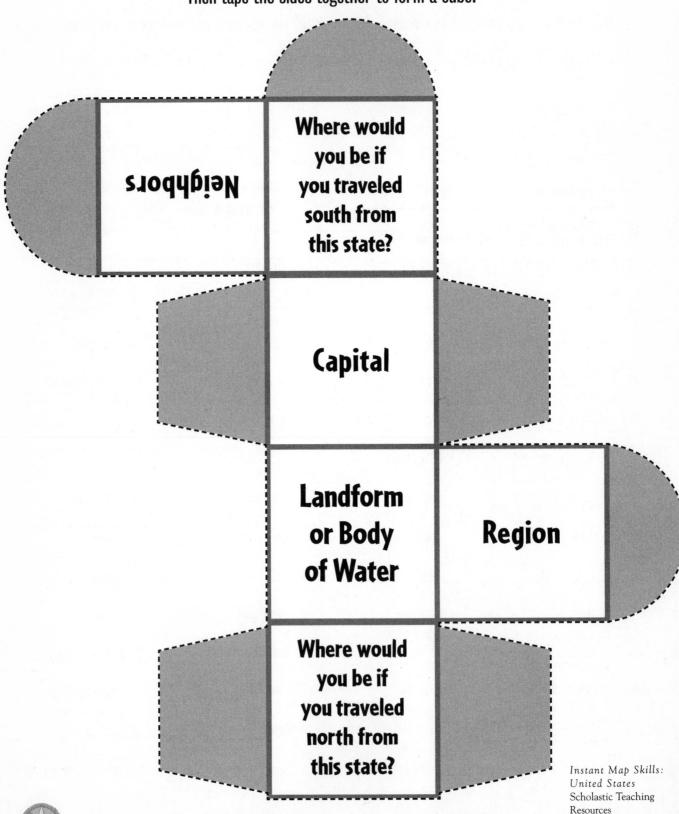

Neighbors

Where would you be if you traveled south from this state?

Capital

Landform or Body of Water

Region

Where would you be if you traveled north from this state?

Instant Map Skills:
United States
Scholastic Teaching
Resources

Where Am I?

Our traveler is confused. Use the wall map to help him figure out where he is.

1. I'm visiting the state that shares the most borders with other states. Where am I?

_____

2. I'm in the state that shares no borders with other states or countries. Where am I?

_____

3. I'm in the easternmost capital city in the U.S. Where am I?

_____

4. I'm in the northernmost state that's shaped like a rectangle. Where am I?

_____

5. I started in the state with the longest coastline. Then I traveled north into the next state. Where am I?

_____

6. I started in the state that has coastlines on four of the Great Lakes. Then I traveled to a state that is southeast from the capital of that state. Where am I?

_____

7. I am in a capital city that is almost directly north of Denver, Colorado. Where am I?

_____

8. I am in the northernmost capital city along the Mississippi River. Where am I?

_____

9. I am floating down a river that has four capital cities located on it. Where am I?

_____

10. I am in a capital city located on a large lake. Where am I?

_____

States & Capitals Bingo

Kansas	Vermont	Alaska	Oklahoma	Arkansas
Arizona	Rhode Island	Iowa	Tennessee	Illinois
Connecticut	North Carolina	★	West Virginia	Louisiana
Georgia	Nebraska	Colorado	Utah	Mississippi
Alabama	New York	Wyoming	Oregon	New Jersey

States & Capitals Bingo

Nevada	Delaware	Kentucky	Virginia	Arizona
Missouri	Alaska	Ohio	Wisconsin	Florida
Louisiana	Texas	★	California	Massachusetts
Idaho	Oregon	Maryland	Indiana	New Mexico
Colorado	North Dakota	Hawaii	Minnesota	South Carolina

States & Capitals Bingo

Illinois	Florida	Hawaii	Iowa	New Hampshire
Michigan	Arizona	Maryland	Arkansas	Massachusetts
Kansas	Washington	★	Kentucky	Montana
Georgia	South Dakota	Maine	Idaho	Connecticut
California	Wyoming	Pennsylvania	Wisconsin	Mississippi

States & Capitals Bingo

Nebraska	South Dakota	Washington	Tennessee	Montana
Pennsylvania	New York	Virginia	Rhode Island	New Jersey
Oklahoma	North Carolina	★	Ohio	North Dakota
Indiana	New Mexico	Vermont	South Carolina	New Hampshire
Missouri	West Virginia	Utah	Kentucky	Nevada

States & Capitals Bingo

Card 1

Montana	New Mexico	North Dakota	Ohio	New Hampshire
Utah	Alabama	Texas	Oregon	Oklahoma
Pennsylvania	South Dakota	★	Rhode Island	South Carolina
Mississippi	Tennessee	Minnesota	Massachusetts	Michigan
Nevada	New Jersey	North Carolina	New York	Nebraska

States & Capitals Bingo

Card 2

California	Georgia	Virginia	Florida	Colorado
Kansas	Maryland	Vermont	Maine	Iowa
Michigan	Illinois	★	Indiana	Louisiana
Delaware	Washington	Utah	West Virginia	Connecticut
Wisconsin	Hawaii	Texas	Idaho	Wyoming

States & Capitals Bingo

Card 3

Wisconsin	Connecticut	Florida	Delaware	Alabama
Colorado	Louisiana	Kentucky	Iowa	California
Maryland	Kansas	★	Minnesota	Maine
Arkansas	Missouri	Michigan	Indiana	Arizona
Alaska	Idaho	Georgia	Hawaii	Wyoming

States & Capitals Bingo

Card 4

Minnesota	Nevada	North Carolina	New York	New Hampshire
Pennsylvania	Virginia	Oregon	Rhode Island	Oklahoma
Washington	Vermont	★	Utah	Texas
North Dakota	South Carolina	Ohio	Tennessee	South Dakota
New Jersey	New Mexico	Nebraska	Montana	Missouri

States & Capitals Bingo

Frankfort	Boston	Phoenix	St. Paul	Montgomery
Atlanta	Tallahassee	Dover	Hartford	Jackson
Indianapolis	Springfield	★	Boise	Honolulu
Olympia	Baton Rouge	Sacramento	Topeka	Des Moines
Denver	Juneau	Lansing	Little Rock	Annapolis

States & Capitals Bingo

Frankfort	Albany	Des Moines	Indianapolis	Springfield
Lansing	Boston	Annapolis	Helena	Baton Rouge
Augusta	Jefferson City	★	Pierre	St. Paul
Providence	Harrisburg	Hartford	Tallahassee	Lincoln
Oklahoma City	Columbus	Bismarck	Raleigh	Topeka

States & Capitals Bingo

Jefferson City	Columbia	Lincoln	Carson City	Montpelier
Nashville	Santa Fe	Olympia	Raleigh	Bismarck
Columbus	Oklahoma City	★	Salem	Harrisburg
Providence	Helena	Pierre	Trenton	Austin
Salt Lake City	Concord	Richmond	Albany	Charleston

States & Capitals Bingo

Phoenix	Dover	Juneau	Topeka	St. Paul
Baton Rouge	Augusta	Annapolis	Boston	Lansing
Frankfort	Jackson	★	Jefferson City	Charleston
Salt Lake City	Montgomery	Des Moines	Madison	Little Rock
Sacramento	Denver	Hartford	Cheyenne	Santa Fe

States & Capitals Bingo

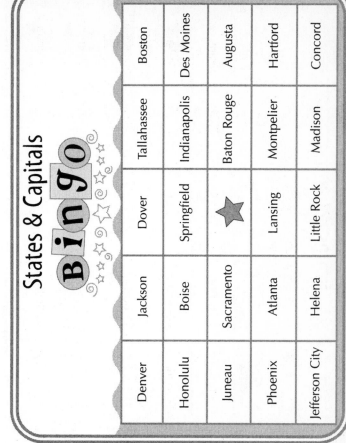

Phoenix	Madison	Trenton	Santa Fe	Honolulu
Raleigh	Bismarck	Columbus	Oklahoma City	Salem
Richmond	Providence	★	Olympia	Pierre
Nashville	Austin	Salt Lake City	Montpelier	Harrisburg
Columbia	Charleston	Concord	Cheyenne	Montgomery

States & Capitals Bingo

Denver	Jackson	Dover	Tallahassee	Boston
Honolulu	Boise	Springfield	Indianapolis	Des Moines
Juneau	Sacramento	★	Baton Rouge	Augusta
Phoenix	Atlanta	Lansing	Montpelier	Hartford
Jefferson City	Helena	Little Rock	Madison	Concord

States & Capitals Bingo

Cheyenne	Springfield	Indianapolis	Montgomery	Topeka
Frankfort	Juneau	Augusta	Annapolis	Little Rock
Tallahassee	Honolulu	★	Jackson	Austin
Helena	Atlanta	Carson City	Concord	Trenton
Santa Fe	Albany	Charleston	Madison	Boise

States & Capitals Bingo

St. Paul	Boise	Olympia	Atlanta	Sacramento
Pierre	Harrisburg	Salem	Santa Fe	Austin
Raleigh	Bismarck	★	Columbus	Oklahoma City
Trenton	Harrisburg	Providence	Columbia	Carson City
Nashville	Albany	Salt Lake City	Montpelier	Richmond

Call List   States and Capitals Bingo

Group 1

		Illinois	Massachusetts	New Hampshire	Oregon	Vermont
		Indiana	Michigan	New Jersey	Pennsylvania	Virginia
Alabama	Connecticut	Iowa	Minnesota	New Mexico	Rhode Island	Washington
Alaska	Delaware	Kansas	Mississippi	New York	South Carolina	West Virginia
Arizona	Florida	Kentucky	Missouri	North Carolina	South Dakota	Wisconsin
Arkansas	Georgia	Louisiana	Montana	North Dakota	Tennessee	Wyoming
California	Hawaii	Maine	Nebraska	Ohio	Texas	
Colorado	Idaho	Maryland	Nevada	Oklahoma	Utah	

Group 2

		Springfield	Boston	Concord	Salem	Montpelier
		Indianapolis	Lansing	Trenton	Harrisburg	Richmond
Montgomery	Hartford	Des Moines	St. Paul	Santa Fe	Providence	Olympia
Juneau	Dover	Topeka	Jackson	Albany	Columbia	Charleston
Phoenix	Tallahassee	Frankfort	Jefferson City	Raleigh	Pierre	Madison
Little Rock	Atlanta	Baton Rouge	Helena	Bismarck	Nashville	Cheyenne
Sacramento	Honolulu	Augusta	Lincoln	Columbus	Austin	
Denver	Boise	Annapolis	Carson City	Oklahoma City	Salt Lake City	

Instant Map Skills: United States   Scholastic Teaching Resources

All About Landforms

Flip Book

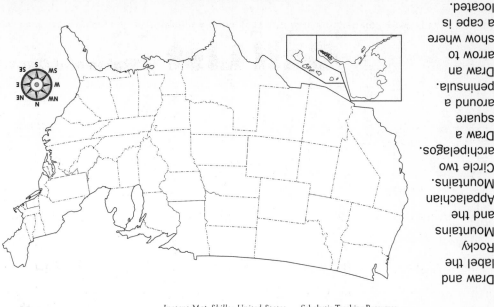

Draw and label the Rocky Mountains and the Appalachian Mountains. Circle two archipelagos. Draw a square around a peninsula. Draw an arrow to show where a cape is located.

Cape & Peninsula

A cape is land that projects or extends into an ocean, sea, gulf, bay, or lake. Draw a picture of a cape in the box.

A peninsula is land that projects or extends into an ocean, sea, gulf, bay, or lake. Draw a picture of a peninsula in the box.

Think you know all about landforms? Use the clues below to complete the crossword puzzle.

Island & Archipelago

A hill is a rounded, raised landform. It is smaller than a mountain. Draw a picture of a hill in the box.

A mountain is a high, rounded or pointed landform with steep sides. It is larger than a hill. Draw a picture of a mountain.

An archipelago is a group of islands. Draw a picture of an archipelago in the box.

A Landform Puzzle

Hill ◆ Mountain ◆ Volcano ◆ Butte ◆ Mesa ◆ Plateau

A peninsula is land that is surrounded by water on three sides. Draw a picture of a peninsula in the box.

Across

4. What you call land that is surrounded by water on three sides.

5. A raised and rounded landform.

Down

1. Land that is completely surrounded by water.

2. The Rockies are an example of this landform.

3. This landform can erupt.

An island is land that is completely surrounded by water. Draw a picture of an island in the box.

A plateau is a high, flat landform that rises steeply above the surrounding land. A plateau is larger than a mesa and a butte. Draw a picture of a mesa.

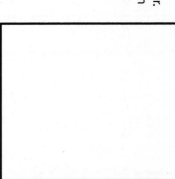

A volcano is an opening in the earth through which lava, rock, and gases are forced out. Draw a picture of a volcano in the box.

A butte is a small, flat-topped hill. A butte is smaller than a mesa or a plateau. Draw a picture of a butte in the box.

A mesa is a high, flat landform rising steeply above the surrounding land. A mesa is larger than a butte but smaller than a plateau. Draw a picture of a mesa here.

Name _____   Date _____

Mountain Peaks in the U.S.A.

The map below shows some of the highest peaks in the United States.
Use the map to answer the questions below.

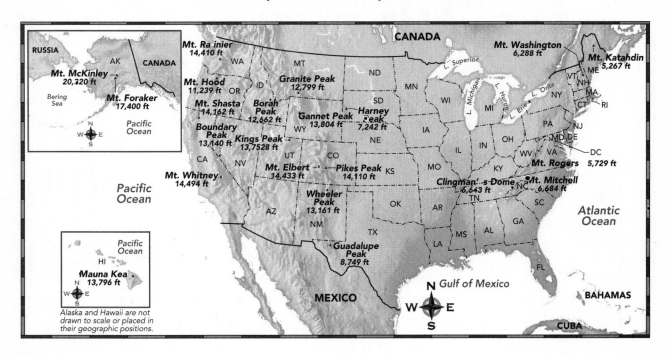

1. What is the tallest mountain in the United States?_____
   In which state is it located?_____

2. What is the highest mountain east of the Mississippi River? _____
   How tall is it? _____

3. Are the Rocky Mountains or the Appalachian Mountains higher? _____
   How can you tell? _____

4. What is the highest mountain in Hawaii? _____ How tall is it? _____

5. Which mountain is named after our first president?_____
   In which state is it located?_____

6. Which mountain is in California?_____
   How high is it? _____

A Weather Map

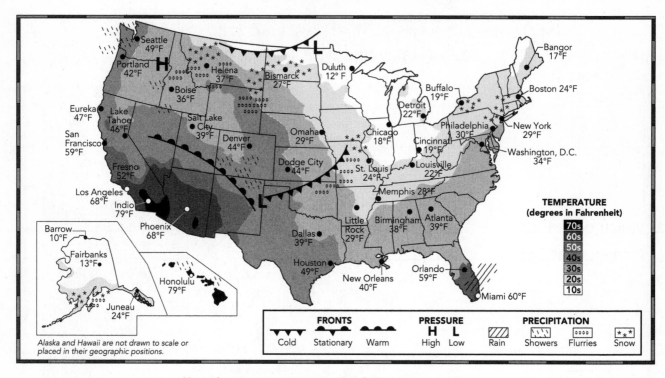

Use the map to answer the following questions.

1. Which three states have the warmest temperatures? _____

2. Which state has the coldest temperatures? _____

3. What is the average temperature in South Carolina? _____

4. What is the temperature in Duluth, Minnesota? _____

5. Which part of Arkansas is warmer? _____

6. The west part of Wyoming has high mountains. How does this affect the

temperatures there? _____

7. How many different temperature zones are there along the Atlantic Ocean? _____
What do you notice about these zones as you move south? _____

8. Describe the weather in Bismarck, North Dakota? _____

Instant Map Skills: United States   Scholastic Teaching Resources

Latitude and Longitude

Use the map of
California to answer
questions about
latitude and
longitude.

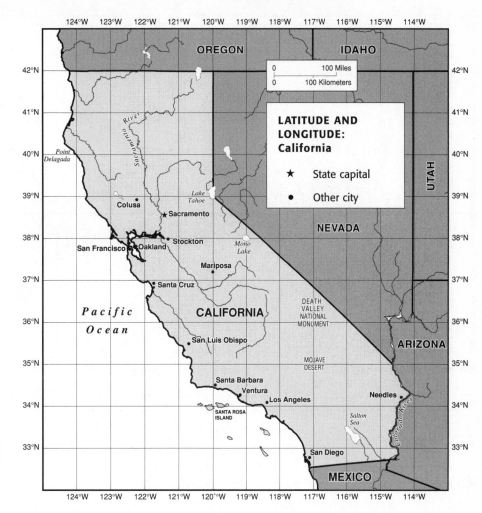

LATITUDE AND
LONGITUDE:
California

★   State capital

•   Other city

1. Which desert is
located near 35°N,
117°W?

_____

2. What is the latitude
of Stockton?

_____

3. Which city is located
at 122°W just south
of 39°N?

_____

4. The line 42°N forms the border between California and
which other state? _____

5. What lake is located at 39°N, 120°W? _____

6. What is the latitude and longitude of Santa Rosa Island? _____

7. What is the latitude and longitude of Mono Lake? _____

8. What city is located near 34°N, 118°W? _____

Instant Map Skills: United States   Scholastic Teaching Resources

Regions Mini-book

Some of the ways people in this region make a living are:

_____
_____
_____
_____
_____
_____

Important cities in this region are:

_____
_____
_____
_____
_____
_____

Products produced in this region are:

_____
_____
_____
_____
_____
_____

Important landforms in this region are:

_____
_____
_____
_____
_____

Two cool facts about this region are:

1. _____
   _____

2. _____
   _____

Important rivers in this region are:

_____
_____
_____
_____

All About the

(name of region)

The states that make up this region are:

_____
_____
_____
_____

Instant Map Skills: United States   Scholastic Teaching Resources

Name _____   Date _____

Comparing Map Scales

Use the two maps below to answer the questions.
Use a ruler to measure the distances on each map.

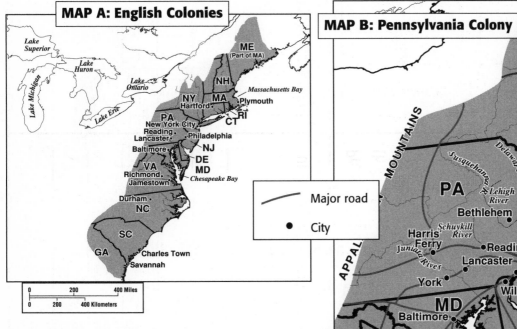

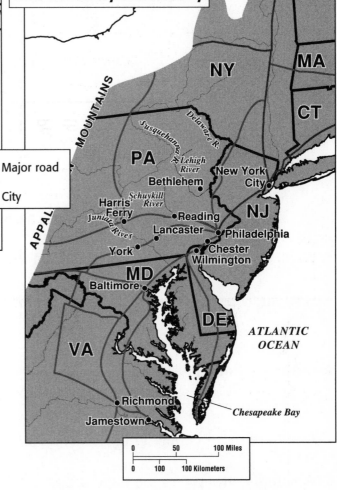

1. On Map A, one inch equals how many
   miles? _____
   On Map B? _____

2. Which map shows a larger area?
   _____

3. Which map shows more detail of
   a smaller area? _____

4. Which map would you use if you
   wanted to compare all of the 13
   English colonies? _____

5. What is the distance from Savannah,
   Georgia, to Jamestown, Virginia?

   _____

6. What is the distance from Harris
   Ferry, Pennsylvania, to Chester,
   Pennsylvania? _____

7. What is the distance from Richmond,
   Virginia, to Chester, Pennsylvania?

   _____

Looking at Population Graphs

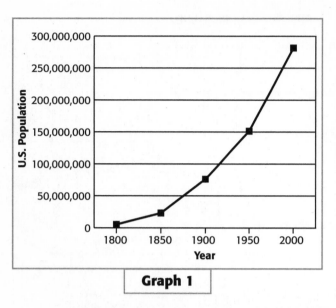

Graph 1

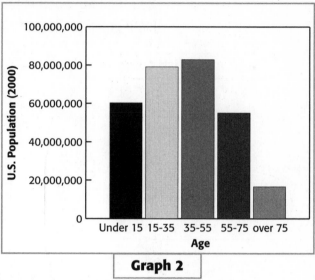

Graph 2

Use the graphs to answer questions about the population in the United States.

1. What was the population of the United States in 1850? _____

2. How many people under the age of 15 were in the United States in 2000?_____

3. Between which years did the population of the United States go over 100 million?

_____

4. Are there more people in the United States over 75 or under 15? _____

5. Which age group has the largest population in the United States in 2000?

_____

6. What was the population of the United States in 1950? _____

7. What was the population of the United States in 2000? _____

8. Which graph shows the change of population over time? _____
What is the time period shown? _____

Instant Map Skills: United States   Scholastic Teaching Resources